SCIENTIFIC AMERICAN | EDUCATIONAL PUBLISHING

SCIENTIFIC AMERICAN INVESTIGATES CAREERS IN SCIENCE

ANTHROPOLOGIST

BY MEGAN QUICK

Published in 2026 by The Rosen Publishing Group
in association with Scientific American Educational Publishing
2544 Clinton Street, Buffalo NY 14224

Library of Congress Cataloging-in-Publication Data
Names: Quick, Megan, author.
Title: Anthropologist / Megan Quick.
Description: Buffalo, New York : Scientific American Educational
    Publishing, an imprint of Rosen Publishing, [2026] | Series: Scientific
    American investigates careers in science | Includes index. | Audience:
    Grades 4-6
Identifiers: LCCN 2024058727 (print) | LCCN 2024058728 (ebook) | ISBN
    9781725352506 (lib. bdg.) | ISBN 9781725352490 (paperback) | ISBN
    9781725352513 (ebook)
Subjects: LCSH: Anthropologists–Juvenile literature. | Human beings–Study
    and teaching–Juvenile literature. | Anthropology–Vocational
    guidance–Juvenile literature.
Classification: LCC GN31.5 .Q53 2026 (print) | LCC GN31.5 (ebook) | DDC
    301–dc23/eng/20250108
LC record available at https://lccn.loc.gov/2024058727
LC ebook record available at https://lccn.loc.gov/2024058728

Designer: Leslie Taylor
Editor: Megan Quick

Portions of this work were originally authored by Jill Keppeler and published as *Be an Anthropologist*. All new material in this edition is authored by Megan Quick.

Photo credits: Cover (main) Microgen/Shutterstock.com; series art (background) jijomathaidesigners/Shutterstock.com; p. 5 Xavier Lorenzo/Shutterstock.com; p. 7 Ababsolutum/iStockphoto.com; p. 8 HelloRF Zcool/Shutterstock.com; p. 9 Godot13/File:School children (Lukhanyo Primary School, Zwelihle Township (Hermanus, South Africa) 02.jpg_commons. wikimedia.org; p. 10 favorita1987/Shutterstock.com; p. 13 steve estvanik/Shutterstock.com; p. 15 Designua/Shutterstock. com; p. 17 IFTN/Alamy.com; p. 19 Sergio Azenha/Alamy.com; p. 20 Frame Stock Footag\e/Shutterstock.com; p. 21 microgen/iStockphoto.com; p. 23 Anton Chalakov/Shutterstock.com; p. 24 Jeff Walker/Flickr.com; p. 25 Shaan Hurley/Flickr. com; p. 26 SurfsUp/Shutterstock.com; p. 27 Photobank.kiev.ua/Shutterstock.com; p. 29 Anton_Ivanov/Shutterstock.com.

Some of the images in this book illustrate individuals who are models. The depictions do not imply actual situations or events.

Printed in the United States of America

CPSIA compliance information: Batch #CSSA26. For Further Information contact Rosen Publishing at 1-800-237-9932.

Find us on 

CONTENTS

Words in the glossary appear in **bold** type the first time they are used in the text.

UNDERSTANDING HUMANS

Have you ever visited another country, or seen people from another country on television? They may have dressed, talked, or acted differently than you do. They have their own **culture**.

Have you visited a zoo and watched chimpanzees? You may have seen them interact with each other in a way that seemed almost human. That's because people and chimps are closely related.

These two subjects may seem very different, but they're both areas studied by anthropologists. There are two main fields in the science of anthropology: cultural and physical. The goal of both is to understand humans and why they live and act the way they do.

Anthropologists study the
differences among people as well
as what they have in common.

THE SCIENCE OF CULTURE

Cultural anthropologists study human cultures and **societies** and how these cultures and societies came to be. Their goal is to discover why people do certain things and why they have certain beliefs. Cultural anthropology is a social science, which means it deals with society and behavior, or how people act.

Cultural anthropologists look at what societies have in common, the differences between them, and why these similarities and differences exist. They study what people think is important and the rules they have for their lives. They often study customs, or the way of doing things that is usual among the people in a certain group or place.

FUN FACT
EVERY CULTURE HAS DIFFERENT BELIEFS AND CUSTOMS. IN VENEZUELA, IT'S POLITE TO BE A BIT LATE. PEOPLE IN EGYPT DO NOT ASK FOR SALT ON THEIR FOOD. IN GREECE, CHILDREN WHO LOSE A TOOTH THROW IT OFF THE ROOF.

Bowing as a greeting is a Japanese custom. In other cultures, people greet each other with handshakes or kisses.

Cultural anthropology includes many different subjects. Cultural anthropologists may study religion or music. They can also examine art, folklore, law, or **technology**. These subjects apply to all cultures, from ones in out-of-the way places to ones in the middle of cities.

Early cultural anthropologists studied societies and compared them to their own culture. They often viewed their culture as superior, or better. They believed other cultures were very simple, without much to offer. But starting in the 1900s, more anthropologists started believing in the ideas of cultural relativism. This means appreciating and studying each culture without comparing it to or judging it based on other cultures.

Culture and Medicine

Medical anthropologists study the link between health and culture. How do different cultures view health? What do they think about doctors or other medical workers? What part does religion play in their healthcare? By answering questions like these, anthropologists can help those in medicine have a greater understanding of their patients.

MANY VOICES

A major part of any group's culture is their language. Linguistic anthropologists study language in a culture, from the words they use to how people **communicate** with one another. Linguistic anthropologists may study dialects, or the forms of a language that are spoken in different areas, and how these dialects form. They also study how language affects societies and cultures.

Sometimes these anthropologists live as part of the society they're studying so they can observe what people say as they do certain things. They may record a person's voice as they talk to them. They ask people to speak about their culture and lives.

Some linguistic anthropologists study languages that are dying out, including many Native American languages. These schoolchildren are learning the language of the Chemehuevi Indian Tribe.

Wahi'
Waqat
Čiλaaqu'
Wičit

THE HUMAN JOURNEY

Physical anthropologists study the **biology** of human beings. They try to learn more about where we came from. They study fossils and compare the **genes** of animals and people from different places and times. Physical anthropology is considered a natural science, which means it deals with matter.

Some physical anthropologists study how humans evolved, or changed over time, from earlier forms of life. This includes both humans and nonhumans. They might use the fossils of early humans and animals to examine their brain size and other features. Other times, they study animals related to us that are still alive, such as other **primates**, like chimpanzees. They learn about humans living in different parts of the world too.

Sahelanthropus tchadensis

Human history has many branches that go back millions of years.

 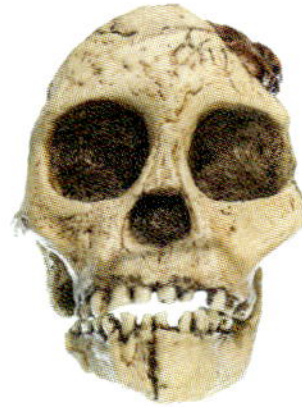  

Australopithecus africanus

Homo erectus

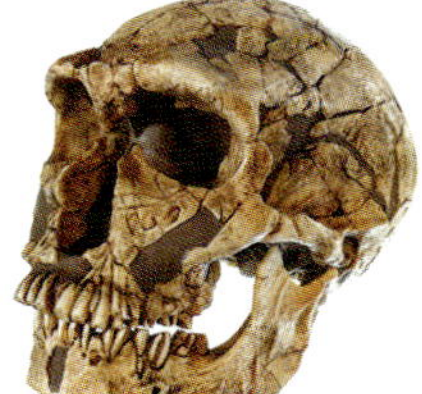

Homo neanderthalensis

Homo sapiens

Studying Skills

Physical anthropologists learn a great deal from studying the fossils of human skulls. The skull can reveal a prehistoric human's health, sex, and appearance. The size of the skull gives the scientist an idea of brain size and how it's changed over time. The position of the skull can indicate whether the human walked on two feet.

IT'S ALL IN THE GENES

Our genes make us who we are. We may have our mother's eyes, our father's smile, or our grandfather's freckles. This is largely thanks to our genes. Some physical anthropologists study DNA, a part of the body that carries genetic information.

You can't see DNA with the naked eye. You need a microscope and other tools in a laboratory. Anthropologists might study how our DNA has changed from the time of earlier humans to now. Or they might compare the DNA in humans from different areas of the world. Anthropologists may also look at how the DNA in humans is the same or different than other animals.

DNA and Genes

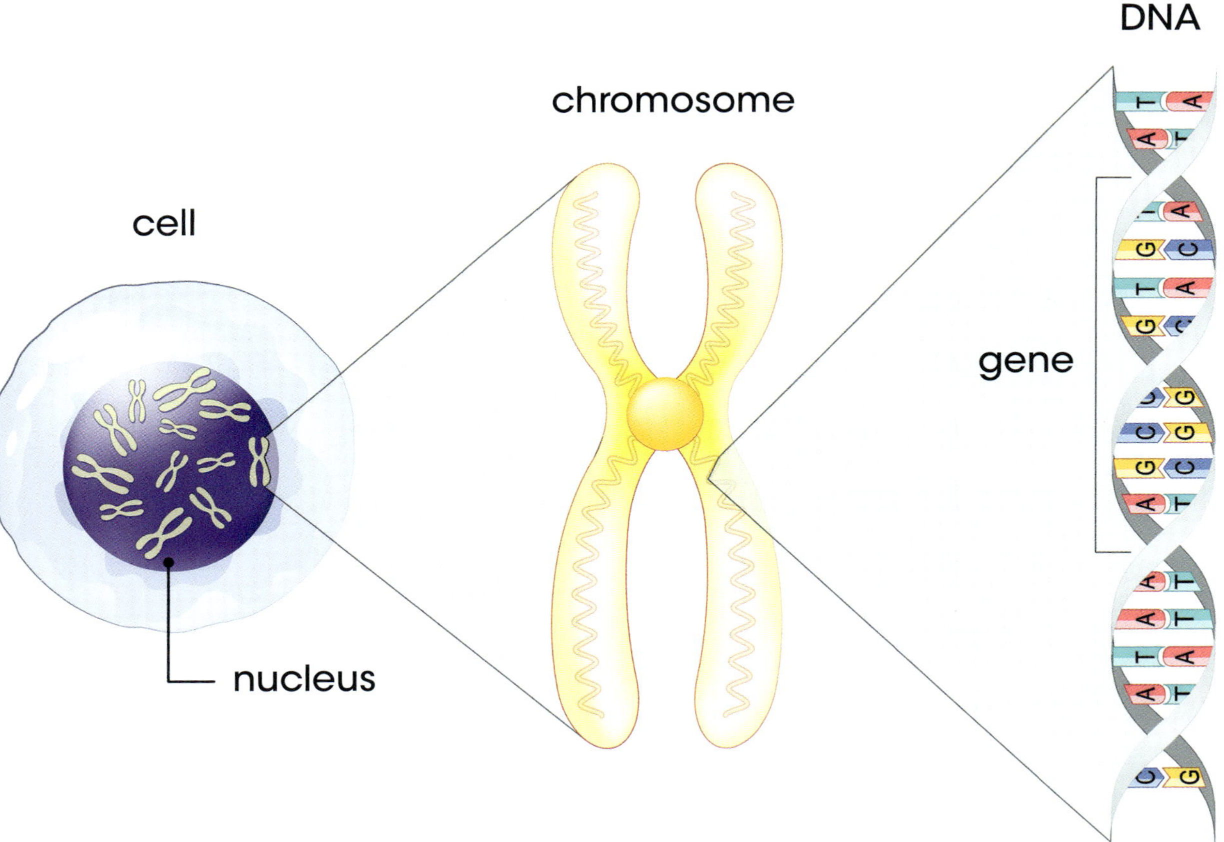

LEARNING FROM CHIMPS

The study of DNA has led to many interesting discoveries. For example, scientists have found that humans and chimpanzees share more than 96 percent of their DNA. Some anthropologists study chimps and other animals closely related to humans. They look at the behavior and physical makeup of our fellow primates to hopefully learn more about our common **ancestors**. We may also learn things that could help save primates in danger and protect humans as well.

For many years, anthropologist Jane Goodall lived with wild chimpanzees in Tanzania, Africa. Goodall's studies showed that the chimpanzees make and use tools. Before this, people thought only humans did this.

FUN FACT

LIKE HUMANS, CHIMP MOTHERS AND CHILDREN HAVE A STRONG BOND. GOODALL EVEN SAW BABY CHIMPS BE ADOPTED BY OTHERS IN THE CHIMP COMMUNITY WHEN THEIR MOTHER DIED.

Goodall's Work

Jane Goodall left her home in England when she was 26 and traveled to Tanzania to study chimpanzees living in the Gombe Stream Game Reserve. She became accepted by the chimps and was able to closely observe their behaviors. She learned that the chimps had social groups and communicated through different sounds.

BONES AS CLUES

Many physical anthropologists study human **remains** in order to learn how humans lived in the past. But forensic anthropologists have a different interest: how people died. By studying a dead person's bones, they can figure out who the person was as well as how and when they died.

A forensic anthropologist might help the police recover and identify human remains, as well as figure out what happened to victims of a crime. In the case of a crime, forensic anthropologists may have to speak in court as witnesses, telling a judge or jury what they learned from a body.

Body Farms

If you decide to study forensic anthropology, you may spend time at an outdoor **research** laboratory known as a body farm. These labs allow students to study actual dead bodies to learn how they decompose, or break down. Students are taught how to identify the body's age, sex, background, and time and cause of death.

Forensic anthropologists use different types of technology in their study of human remains. They often begin by taking photos of the bones as well as X-rays. They might also run a CT scan of the bones, which is like an X-ray, but gives a more detailed image. An anthropologist may study bones with a powerful microscope as well.

What can a forensic anthropologist learn about a crime from these tests? Studying bones and teeth can reveal the person's age, health, and background. Studying the condition of bones can tell them what happened at the time of death. Anthropologists work with a team that includes coroners, who are officials that look into causes of death.

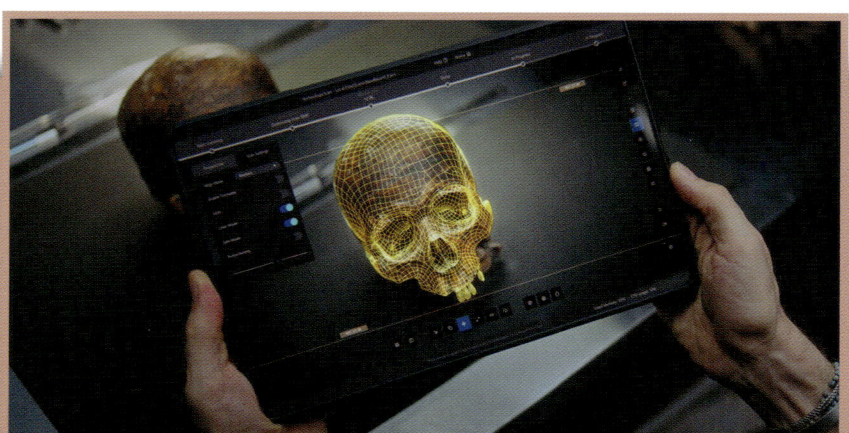

A forensic anthropologist examines remains of a skeleton under a microscope, which lets scientists see objects that are too tiny to see otherwise.

DIGGING UP ANSWERS

We can learn a lot about people who lived long ago from the items they used in their daily lives. Archaeology is branch of anthropology that studies past human life through what people left behind. There are two main types of archaeology: historic and prehistoric. Prehistoric archaeology studies the time before humans started writing down history. Historic archaeology looks at more recent centuries, when people began keeping track of their history.

Archaeologists study **artifacts** left by earlier cultures and try to figure out how those cultures worked. They look at artifacts in historical contexts, or the conditions in which they were made.

Here, archaeologists work at an
excavation site in Bulgaria.

Archaeologists may spend some of their time out in the field, excavating artifacts for study. For archaeologists, fieldwork is discovering and recording archaeological sites and examining what they find there.

It is very important for archaeologists to describe and **classify** the artifacts they find. If an archaeologist can understand the meaning and purpose of an artifact, they can increase our understanding of the past.

An archaeologist may study the earliest human tools—or even more recent technology! They often learn information from a variety of things, such as digging sticks used by early humans or the first cell phones of the 1970s.

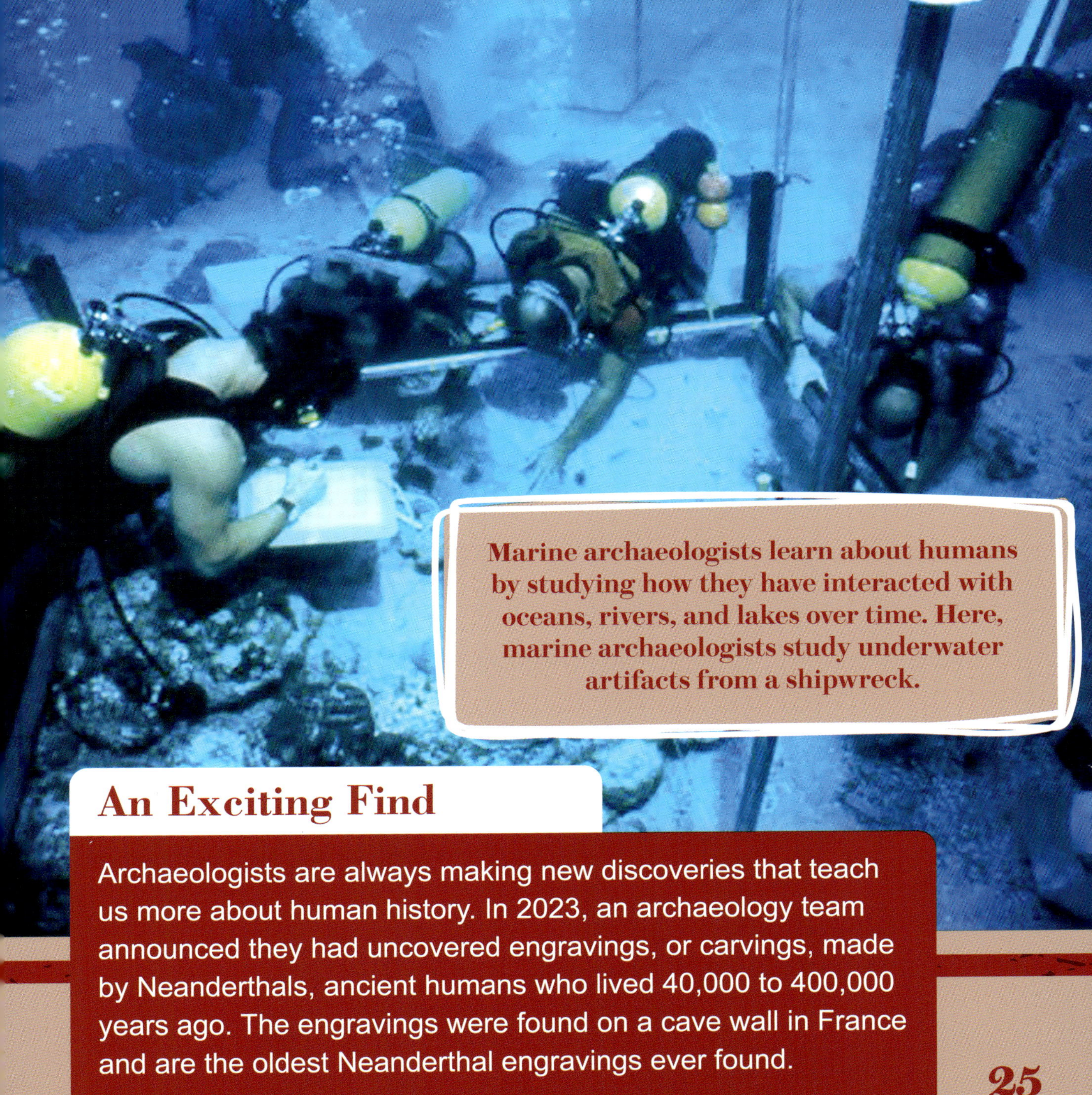

Marine archaeologists learn about humans by studying how they have interacted with oceans, rivers, and lakes over time. Here, marine archaeologists study underwater artifacts from a shipwreck.

An Exciting Find

Archaeologists are always making new discoveries that teach us more about human history. In 2023, an archaeology team announced they had uncovered engravings, or carvings, made by Neanderthals, ancient humans who lived 40,000 to 400,000 years ago. The engravings were found on a cave wall in France and are the oldest Neanderthal engravings ever found.

START STUDYING

Are you thinking about a career in anthropology? If you have an interest in history and different kinds of people, then it might be a good fit for you. The first step toward reaching your goal is to work hard in school.

You'll want to start out in high school by taking classes in history and social studies. From there, you can study and learn more to narrow down what area sounds most interesting to you. You'll benefit from courses in math, languages, and physical sciences, such as biology. Computer classes will also be very helpful. You can major in anthropology when you get to college.

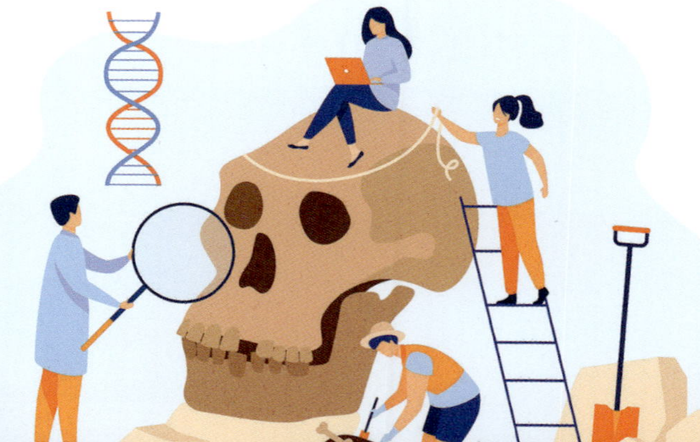

College anthropology classes may give
you the chance for hands-on learning.

CHOOSING YOUR CAREER

There are lots of organizations that hire anthropologists. **Universities** hire anthropologists to teach and do research in laboratories or in the field. Archaeologists as well as forensic and cultural anthropologists may work for the government. Companies use anthropologists to better understand their customers as well as their own workers.

When it comes to careers in anthropology, there are plenty of choices! You can dig up artifacts or study prehistoric customs. You might want to help solve crimes or learn about people of different backgrounds. The science of anthropology provides many ways of understanding humans through time and throughout the world.

Anthropologists work to uncover the stories and history of people from different times and cultures, like these children who live in a village in Rajasthan, India.

GLOSSARY

ancestor: A family member who lived long before you.

artifact: Something made by humans in the past.

biology: A branch of knowledge that deals with living organisms and life processes.

classify: To assign something to a category or class based on shared qualities.

communicate: To share ideas and feelings through sounds and motions.

culture: The beliefs and ways of life of a group of people.

genes: Tiny parts of a cell that are passed along from parent to child and that decide specific features in the child, such as eye color.

primate: Any member of the group of animals that includes humans, apes, and monkeys.

remains: Whatever is left over or behind. Also, a dead body.

research: The collecting of information about a subject.

society: The people who live together in an organized community with traditions, laws, and values.

technology: The way people do something using tools and the tools that they use.

university: A school that offers courses leading to a degree and where research is done.

FOR MORE INFORMATION

Books

Klepeis, Alicia. *Jane Goodall*. Minneapolis, MN: Kids Core, 2022.

Morlock, Rachael. *Respecting Our Differences*. Buffalo, NY: PowerKids Press, 2023.

Sockin, Caitlin. *Dig It!: Archaeology for Kids*. Cary, NC: Persnickety Press, 2023.

Websites

American Museum of Natural History: Anthropology
www.amnh.org/explore/ology/anthropology
Find out about people from different times and cultures through fun activities.

Britannica Kids: Anthropology
kids.britannica.com/kids/article/anthropology/399339
Learn more about physical and cultural anthropology.

What Does It Mean to Be Human?
Humanorigins.si.edu/evidence/human-fossils/mystery-skull-interactive
This interactive page invites you to identify skulls of early human species.

INDEX